IMAGES
*of America*

# HICKMAN
# COUNTY

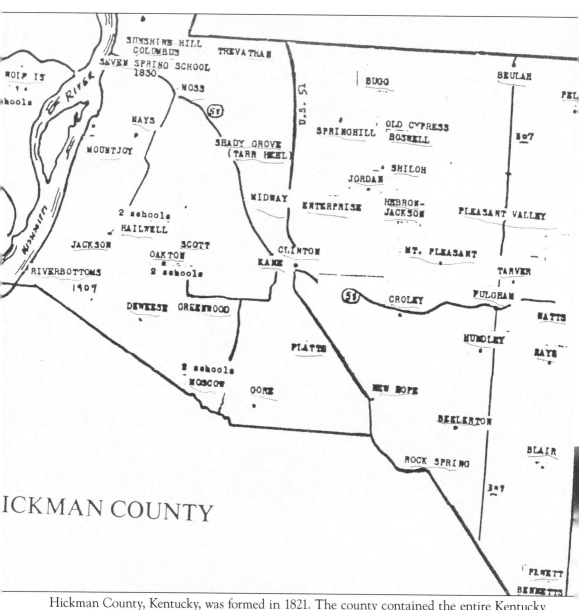

Hickman County, Kentucky, was formed in 1821. The county contained the entire Kentucky portion of the Jackson Purchase. By 1886, Hickman County had been subdivided into eight counties. It is bounded by the Mississippi River on the west, Carlisle County on the north, Graves County on the east, and Fulton County and a mile stretch of Tennessee on the south. (Courtesy of the Hickman County Historical and Genealogical Society.)

ON THE COVER: The Barclay Barber Shop was located under the Clinton Bank Building that stood on the corner of Washington and East Clay Streets. It was owned and managed by Homer Barclay. The shop was first located in the first building east of the bank, and in 1930, Homer bought the Lindsey Jackson shop in the bank basement. The barbers from left to right are Parker Barclay, Len Barclay, Homer Barclay, and Leamon Barclay. Customers could not only get a haircut and shave, but one could have his shoes shined by Albert "Puddin" Rhodes and, on Saturday night, even take a bath. (Courtesy of the author.)

IMAGES
*of America*

# HICKMAN
# COUNTY

LaDonna Latham and
the Hickman County Historical
and Genealogical Society

ARCADIA
PUBLISHING

Copyright © 2010 by LaDonna Latham and the Hickman County Historical and
Genealogical Society
ISBN 978-1-5316-4378-2

Published by Arcadia Publishing
Charleston SC, Chicago IL, Portsmouth NH, San Francisco CA


Library of Congress Control Number: 2009933489

For all general information contact Arcadia Publishing at:
Telephone 843-853-2070
Fax 843-853-0044
E-mail sales@arcadiapublishing.com
For customer service and orders:
Toll-Free 1-888-313-2665

Visit us on the Internet at www.arcadiapublishing.com

*This book is dedicated to all those who have gone
before us and to those who will come after us.*

# CONTENTS

# ACKNOWLEDGMENTS

The Hickman County Historical and Genealogical Society would like to say thank you to all of those who in any way helped with loaning pictures to us, those who made copies, those who mailed them to the society, and those who contributed information about them for this book. We could not have had this book for future generations if these people had not helped.

We are very grateful to the *Hickman County Gazette* for letting us use several of their pictures that were found in copies of old *Gazettes*.

Unless otherwise noted, all images appear courtesy of the Hickman County Historical and Genealogical Society.

Also a special thank-you goes to Norma Gene Humphreys and Wanda Moon for their dedication in helping to make this book a reality.

# INTRODUCTION

In 1783, the Legislature of Virginia began to authorize the "laying of land warrants" along the Mississippi River for the benefit of the soldiers who had served in the Revolutionary War. The first of these warrants was laid on the Mississippi in what is now Hickman County.

In 1816, Kentucky's lieutenant governor, Gabriel Slaughter, pointed out that the land between the Tennessee and Mississippi Rivers still belonged to the Chickasaw Indians. So in 1817, the legislature asked Congress to buy the land and Isaac Shelby and Andrew Jackson were assigned the task of negotiating the sale. The United States would pay the Chickasaw $20,000 per year for 15 years.

The treaty between the commissioners and Chickasaw Chief Chinnubby and his chiefs, headmen, and warriors was signed on October 19, 1818, at Chickasaw Old Town, Mississippi. Kentucky's entire share of land was organized as Hickman County.

Hickman County was the "mother" of all the Jackson Purchase counties. It has been divided into eight different counties since it was organized. Hickman County is the 71st county of Kentucky's 120 counties. It lies in the southwestern part of the state and encompasses 225 square miles. It was named for Capt. Paschal Hickman, a Kentuckian massacred by Native Americans following the Battle of the River Raisin.

The earliest visitors to this area were hunters, surveyors, trappers, and then men wanting land of their own. The settlers flocked to the area, claimed their piece of land, and began to build a new life on this frontier. The earliest settlement was Columbus, with Moscow second, and then Oakton. There were settlements at Clinton, Beulah, St. Denis, Rock Springs, Springhill, Shiloh, Fulgham, and Beelerton.

The land is gently rolling, and the soil is fertile. Hickman County is an agricultural region, and most producers today raise corn, soybeans, or tobacco. There are a few colorful clay deposits in the bluff areas along the river at Columbus. This fine white clay was once used in pottery making.

As much as Hickman County tried to stay neutral during the Civil War, it was an impossible deed. Hickman County's young men were signing up in Columbus to go to war—some to the North and some to the South. Columbus being the northern terminal for the Mobile and Ohio Railroad meant that either side could come into the county. There were several engagements at Columbus, and with Hickman County being strong with Confederate sympathizers, it caused much antagonism.

After the start of the 20th century, Hickman County grew socially, economically, educationally, and culturally. There were factories, new schools, bigger farm enterprises, a movie theater, teen town, and new businesses. Columbus-Belmont State Park was renovated. The county moved from dirt streets to asphalt paving, kerosene lamps to electricity, horse and buggies to the automobile, and from well water to city water. These advancements help the county to grow and prosper.

Today Hickman County's economy has been on a downward spiral. The factories have left or shut down, and so many of the businesses have closed. Our young people have had to go other places to get the high-paying jobs or just a job, period. This has meant that a lot of the buildings have been abandoned or neglected. They eventually fall down or stay in ruin.

The Hickman County Historical and Genealogical Society has published this book in hopes that the future generations will see that Hickman County was once and can be again a thriving community. We hope also they see preserved a bit of the history of Hickman County that was, that is, and we pray will always be.

Court Square, Clinton, Ky., in the early 1900's

This photograph taken in the early 1900s shows the main street of Clinton facing south. In the lower left-hand corner is Bowers Grocery. In later years, the Clinton Bank Building was located on this site until a new building was built on East Clay Street. In the background is the old First Baptist Church, and the courthouse square is on the right side. (Courtesy of Joyce Allen.)

# One

# Businesses

## Merchandise, Trades, Offices, and Specialties

This 1908 image of Main Street or East Clay Street in Clinton shows how life has changed in Hickman County. Clinton has grown from dirt streets to paved roads, from horses and buggies to the automobile. One can also see that some things have stayed the same. Some of the buildings on this street can still be seen as they were 100 years ago with little change, on the outside at least. The inner structures have been changed to meet the needs of the people of today.

These are scenes from the north side of Clinton's courthouse square in 1916 and in 2009. Along what is now called East Clay Street, the buildings on the left have housed grocery stores, clothing stores, a pool hall, drugstores, flower shops, beauty shops, insurance companies, and the Hickman County Historical Society. Most of these buildings have stood from at least 1908 to 2009.

The powerhouse and the water storage tank (the round building) were in the northwest part of Clinton. A water system came about in about 1897, and electricity came to Clinton around 1903. At first, power was said to have been rationed, being turned on from dark until around 10:00 p.m. It was then turned off until the next evening. In later years, ice was delivered by horse and buggy to homes and businesses all around Clinton, or one could come and buy ice in block form or bags of crushed ice. The ice plant section was sold to a New Mexico firm who dismantled it and shipped it to another location in 1950–1951.

These water tanks are located on Highway 51 South and were owned by Kentucky Water Service, Inc. In 1957, the new larger one replaced the small one, which was built in 1897. The old one was removed, and the newer one is still in service. The old tank's capacity was 50,000 gallons, while the newer one was 178,500 gallons. (Courtesy of Jean Yates.)

11

Bugg Brothers Feed and Supply Company was a retail dealership for Purina Feeds and other farm supplies. In 1952, Edward, Howard, and Holly Jr. Bugg opened the business located on Water Street. Even though Holly died in 1959, the partnership continued for several years after. The business is now closed.

These were the employees who could be found working at Star Milling Company. Some have been identified. From left to right are (first row) four unidentified, Joe Payne, Archie Chester Myers (behind Woodford Ringo), Woodford Ringo, unidentified, Imogene Lemond, unidentified, and Urey Patrick; (second row) two unidentified, "Hammerchin" Myers (barely visible), Chester Myers, Glenn Myers, and unidentified; (third row) unidentified. (Courtesy of Agnes Ferguson.)

Log teams can be seen here in 1921–1922 taking their loads to Joe Craddock's sawmill located down the street. They are passing Craddock's Grocery, owned by Simon Craddock, and the Budwine Bottling plant. Who owned the plant is not known today. The roads were dirt and the sidewalks made of planks. The picture below shows Beckham Craddock, 19 years old, who ran the grocery store. (Both courtesy of Gerald Craddock.)

The Clinton Bottling Works was owned by J. W. Lamkin and Cecil Scott. Lamkin started the plant in 1920 while H. W. Weatherford's Whistle Bottling Plant was in production. In 1929, the two plants consolidated, forming the Clinton Bottling Company, and Weatherford and Lamkin were partners. In 1932, Scott purchased Weatherford's interest. In 1933, beer was added to the list of merchandise to be sold. The company was making Cinderella Orange, Club Lemon, Cream, Cherry Blossom, Grape, Peach, and Four Per Cent in 1934. J. D. Williams was the bookkeeper; L. L. Johnson, salesman; Bert Hill, bottler and plant man; Curley Lamkin, utility man; and Arnell Klapp, main bottler and city salesman.

Dempsey Ringo Sr. and Carl A. James formed the Hickman County Feed Mill in 1946. Both had been employees at Star Milling Company before opening their own business. James was the miller who helped farmers with their feeding problems. They ground and mixed the feed according to the individual formula for each patron. When James retired in 1963, Dempsey Ringo Jr. purchased his share of the business. Pictured are Dempsey Ringo Sr. (left) and Dempsey Jr.

In 1942, Sam Harper Jr. took over the Evans-Harper Stockyards, and this partnership was dissolved because of Sam Harper Sr.'s death. Harper Stockyards bought and sold all kinds of livestock. The stockyards were sold to Roy Berry in 1957.

In 1939, Roy Berry leased the old Railroad Stockyards and did business there until he bought the Harper Stockyards in 1957. The office was an old railroad car. Jimmy and Jerry, both sons of Roy, helped in the business at different times. Jerry drove a truck hauling the livestock to such places as Tupelo, Mississippi; Memphis, Tennessee; and St. Louis, Missouri. Jimmy started in the business in 1957 when the Harper Stockyards were bought. They shipped mostly hogs and veal calves. In 1965, Jimmy bought his dad's share of the business and continued to ship cattle and hogs almost daily. (Courtesy of Jimbo Berry.)

The Clinton Depot was for the Illinois Central Railroad. This picture was taken in 1916 and shows a horse-drawn taxi in the foreground. The segregated waiting rooms were on the south side, and the freight area was on the north. The depot agent looked for oncoming trains by using the bay window.

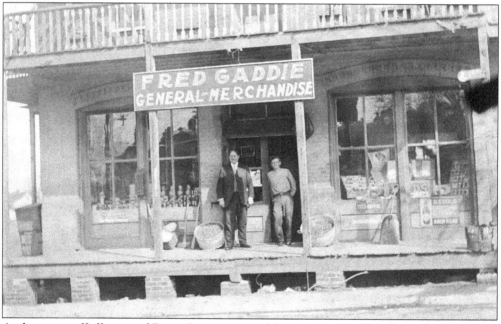

At the corner of Jefferson and Depot Streets, one could stop by Fred Gaddie's General Merchandise Store, later called Five Points Store, and find a well-furnished grocery and mercantile establishment. Shown in the picture are Howard Brummal and Fred Gaddie (in doorway). Gaddie ran the grocery until his death in 1929. Gaddie had been in the grocery business for 35 years. The store then became Joe Stroud's veterinary clinic and restaurant. He and his wife, Radie, ran the business until he retired about 1948–1949. T. C. Maxey started Maxey's Grocery there in 1950.

Located on Highway 51 North was the Clinton Hatchery, which was started by George W. Bacot in January 1928. Bacot sold chicken feed, garden supplies, wire fencing, roofing, fertilizers, and garden seed, as well as baby chicks. Edward Benedict, J. S. Bacot, J. B. Townsend, "Goat" Fait, and Robert McClam were employees in 1953.

This picture shows the inside of the Clinton Hatchery. It was said that this warehouse covered an acre of ground. As one can see, there are plenty of supplies to sell. In the right-hand corner is a "drive through" where customers could drive into the building and load their supplies from the hatchery floor.

Today one can find Jewell Mart North on the same site where the Clinton Hatchery did business. Danny and Joyce Jewell own the business, and their son, Brian, manages it. They sell items such as fried chicken, desserts, candy, gum, gas, and drinks.

This building housed Ned Benedict's blacksmith shop. He was one of the very last blacksmiths in the county, if not the last. Before modern transportation took to the road, he shod horses, repaired wagons and buggies, and sharpened or made lots of different plows and farm implements. In the later years, his job was mainly farm repairs with an occasional horse to be shod. He closed his shop in 1958, and a service station has been built there. At this time, there is nothing there but an empty building. (Courtesy of Annell Orlando.)

Just across the street from the blacksmith shop sat the John Walker Hales Service Station. Patrons could buy gas, have their oil changed, or have other work done on their automobile. He would even wash the car. In March 1956, this picture was made; from left to right are Toby Chester, Raymond Bowden, ? Bostick, and John Walker Hales. The station still stands today, but no one is using it. (Courtesy of Annell Orlando.)

This building was once Faulkner's Harness Shop and then a shoe store. It was located south of Ned Benedict's Blacksmith Shop on Highway 51. It has also housed Eva's Beauty Shop, with Eva Benedict the owner. The little shop was torn down and a brick building was built, which was the home of the Clinton Fire Station. (Courtesy of Annell Orlando.)

On what is now East Clay Street, where the Clinton Bank is now located, was Martinetti's Meat Market. In 1934, they sold beef roast for 10 to 15¢ per pound, and hog lard was 7.5¢ per pound. In 1951, Dr. O. C. Barber started his chiropractor business in the shop.

The Independent Service Station and Garage sat on the same lot as the Clinton Dental Clinic does today. In 1937, Marvin Cunningham was the manager. They sold Plymouth and Desoto automobiles and also were equipped to service any make or model car. Every need of a motorist could be handled at this station.

In 1909, the Clinton Bank opened for business in its new building, which was located on the corner of Washington and East Clay Streets. It had previously been located in a building between the new building and the Farm Bureau Office since 1887. The building was used by Draughon's Junior College and is now standing empty.

The Clinton Bank built a new building at 220 East Clay Street in 1979 and is still doing business there today. Glynn Reid is the president, and Lisa Rushing is vice president. The board consists of Davis Dixon, Robert Neal Black, Bob Williams, Mac Ringo, Bobby Brown, Kenny Ward, and Jerry Peery.

Before World War I, Clinton had its very own Social Club. It could be found over Brummal Brothers Grocery, located on the north side of East Clay Street and the corner of what is now Highway 51. This was the meeting place to see friends, play cards, or just read a book or newspaper. Some of the members came to perform and harmonize on their musical instruments. Those pictured in the foreground are, from left to right, Warren Brummal, Emma Johnson, Ida Scott, LaVada Samuels Johnson, and Flegel Patrick, who is reading the paper. Sitting at the table alone is Claus Freeman. At the back table are Lillie and Quigley Brummal with Jimmy Bowden, the porter. (Courtesy of Jim and Sue Brummal.)

Looking from the center of the east side of the courthouse square, one would see the Ben Franklin Store, owned by O. L. Young and son C. C. ("Peggy"). It opened in 1936 and did a thriving business with a complete line of merchandise priced from 5¢ to $1. After O. L.'s death in 1940, Peggy continued in the business. Cecil "Peggy" Young is the gentleman in the middle of the isle, and his wife, Mildred, is on the right. Others are unidentified.

The Farm Bureau Office now does business where the Ben Franklin Store once was. It moved to this location from the north side of the square in 1986. Wilson Cannon was the agent and retired shortly after the move. Bill Morgan became agent.

Looking on past the Ben Franklin Store's sign, one will see a sign saying "Lunch." That is Red Fostyr's Black Cat Café. Red operated a first-rate café and was well known to home folks as well as tourists. Red contributed the good business to his cook, Don Crawford. Elmer Heaslett was the counterman for the café for several years. The picture shows Red in the white cap.

In 1947, Bill Yates returned to Clinton, where he and his sons, Bobby Sr. and Lawrence, purchased the Clinton Food Locker. It was located on the east side of the courthouse square. It was a grocery with a locker plant in the back for customers to store frozen food. In the early 1950s, home freezers became available, so the lockers were removed and the family sold groceries only. Yates sold the business to Duane Caldwell about 1956 or 1957. Pictured from left to right are unidentified, Bill Yates, Montell Jewell Creason, and Frank Wisz. In later years, the Spinning Wheel—a flower, craft, and gift shop—was located in this building. (Courtesy of Jean Yates.)

The Williams Hardware Store was located in a building beside the food locker. It was built in the early 1920s and later destroyed by fire. Will Williams rebuilt the building and operated the hardware store with his sons W. E. ("Polly") and Egbert until 1981, when Egbert passed away. This is the interior of the store. It sold everything from tricycles to washing machines. In December 1981, Polly sold the store to Richard Williams (no relation). Richard later sold the building to Jeff Canty, and he tore the building down and sold the lot.

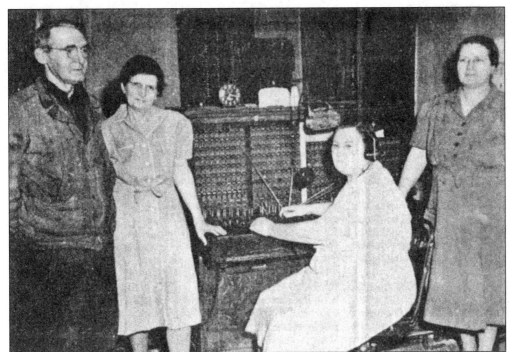

This was the Clinton Rural Telephone Central Office and its workers about 1945. Jim Henderson (left) was the manager. Operators, from left to right, were Fila Berry, Mae Binford, and Tina Davis. The central office served as a general bureau of information. The operator knew where the fire was, where the doctor was and who he was attending, who died and when the funeral was to be held. If anyone wanted to know anything, they just called one of the operators and asked. If she did not know, she knew how to find out.

The Hickman County Court Annex was built in 2005 on the site where Williams Hardware, Featherstone Grocery, and the Rancho Motel were located in earlier years. This building contains the circuit court clerk's office and the courtroom for Hickman County.

In 1901, the Hickman County Bank of Clinton was formed. It operated under this name until 1908, when it became First National Bank of Clinton. The top picture is the second home to the bank. It was located on the southeast corner of the courthouse square. The building was remodeled (as the bottom picture shows), the bank restructured, and the name changed to the First Community Bank with Bruce Kimbell as the president.

In the 1950s, Ann Jackson and Bobbie Jackson Mullins operated Ann and Bobbie's Café. It was located in the building that had once housed the Black Cat Café on the east side of the courthouse square. (Courtesy of Johnny Hobby.)

Hickman County has had five jails. The first was of logs and located in Columbus. The second, also of logs, was built in Clinton in 1832 after the county seat was moved there. This picture is of the third building, erected in 1878. It was located at the corner of South Washington Street and Highway 58 (then known as Mayfield Road). It served the county until 1910–1911, when a fourth jail, made of bricks, was built. It housed prisoners until it was declared substandard in 1991. A new facility was constructed in 1999 on Highway 51 north of Clinton.

The first store on the north side of the square looking west has had a variety of faces in its lifetime. Today it is Perkins Pharmacy, owned by Bobby and Jouella Perkins. In the late 1800s or early 1900s, this was the home of the New York Store, managed by Ben Katz. It has also housed the Kroger Store, Samuels Food Market, and Mendel's Pharmacy.

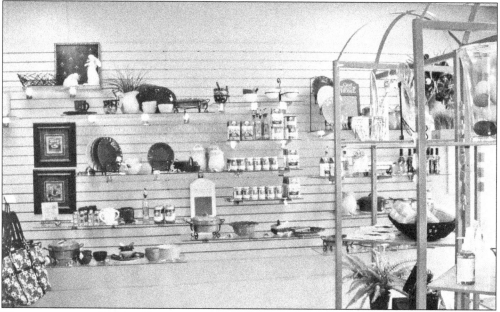

The store next to Perkins Pharmacy is now called ETC and is owned by Scott and Lai Ann Mitchell. They specialize in graduation, baby, anniversary, and wedding gifts. One can also purchase Paula Deen items, such as bottles of spices, cookies, dip mixes, and kitchen items. There are purses, T-shirts, and candles of all fragrances. This was home to the Farm Bureau Office at one time, and it was also home to Emerson's Grocery.

The next building houses two different businesses. The only barbershop left in Clinton is on the east side, with Gilbert Fortner as the barber. He has been barbering for 50 years or more in several different shops around Clinton.

On the west side of the building, one will find what is now First Financial Insurance Services, Inc. In 1987, Jackson Insurance Agency moved in, later to become First Financial. Pictured are Mary Nell Jackson Weatherford and her husband, Jimmy Weatherford, who owned Jackson Insurance Agency. Their daughter, Annell Weatherford Orlando, and Lori Allen are the agents today. (Courtesy of Annell Orlando.)

In 1939, the Kroger store started doing business in the Emerson Hardware Store building. It was in business until 1955, when it was sold to Ray Samuels. Pictured from left to right are Mabel Piper, Jimmy Hodges, and Roy Jackson. (Courtesy of Mabel Piper.)

Waller's Dry Goods Store was located in this building in 1921 when Hubbs Waller, a partner in Flood and Waller, bought Mr. Flood's part of the business. Most goods were seasonal, and clothes came from piece goods. Upstairs on the second-floor balcony, Fay-Rae Beauty Shop was owned and operated by Fay Watts and Rachel Mangrum. The building today houses Shear Blend Beauty Shop, owned by Irvin Stroud and operated by Stroud and Debbie Poole. Tanning beds, manicures, and pedicures—customers can get "the works" at this shop.

Hall Byassee Jr. and Jewell Klapp bought Singletary's Drug Store in 1952. In the Singletary's Drug Store, a customer could have a prescription filled and buy over-the-counter remedies as well as have a soda at the soda fountain with Chink Nall as the operator. In Byassee's, Bill Cross was the operator of the soda fountain. He was still making sodas in the 1960s. Hall Jr. was the pharmacist until Johnny Byassee, Hall's son, became the second-generation owner and operator. He is still filling prescriptions today.

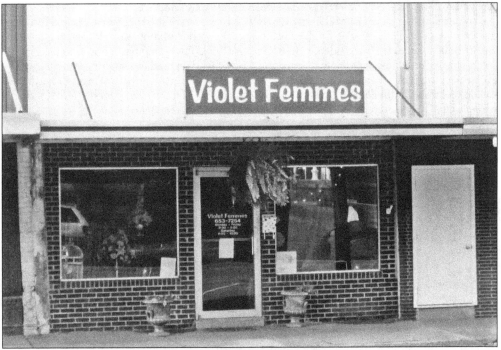

Next door to Byassee Drugs, shoppers can buy floral arrangements, wedding gifts, potted plants, crystal, and other gifts at Violet Femmes. Owner Debbie Armbruster, as well as manager Lauren Armbruster, will be glad to help you make a purchase. In 1919, this building was the home for Jewell Brothers Grocery. Ramer B. and Earl Jewell ran the business for many years. The store was the first to sell bakery-made light bread in Clinton, and in 1927, a meat department was added. The store also had delivery service as late as 1953.

Evelyn Evans donated the two buildings next to Violet Femmes to the Hickman County Historical and Genealogical Society in 1998. The eastern portion of the building was sold, and the revenue was used to remodel the west side for the society in 1999. The group has many records, such as deeds, family group files, wills, marriage records, and other data used in searching for one's family. The society has provided a place where persons interested in genealogy or local history may come and do research. Jimmy Piper's Dollar Store, Ellis Dobson's Dobson's Dry Goods, and Flood and Waller's Dry Goods Store have made this building home to their wares.

This was a business on the north side of the courthouse square but in what building has not been found out. It seems to be a pool hall and restaurant. The men, from left to right, are (behind the counter) Johnson and Biscuit Brummal; (sitting on the stool) Adolf Davidson; (standing) unidentified (with black hat), Jesse McWhorter, unidentified, George Byassee, and ? Weatherford. (Courtesy of Jim and Sue Brummal.)

In 1935, Lawrence "Bill" Yates began as manager of the U-Tote-Em Store in Clinton. The store was located on the northwest corner of West Clay and Jefferson Streets. Bill is second from left above. Below is the store today. R. W. "Tip" Johnson owned a hardware store here until the late 1960s. Billy and Norma Gene Humphreys and Martha and Harold Allison bought the store in 1975 and ran it until 1978, when the Humphreyses sold their part to Martha Allison. She later sold the store to the Witherspoons, who own Clinton Hardware today. (Both courtesy of Jean Yates.)

The Porter Insurance Agency was opened in 1922 as J. A. Porter and Son. Its first location was a small office over Hutcherson Store. They then moved to the Emerson building next to the Strand Theatre. In 1947, they moved once again to Jackson Street. Pictured are, from left to right, Carol Porter, Imogene Milner, Phillip H. Porter, and Roger Schuler, special agent for Hartford Insurance.

In 1992, the Hickman County Ministerial Alliance Committee established a thrift store and the Mission House became a reality. It supplies clothing, furniture, other household supplies, and food at reasonable prices. At Christmas, there is a Toy Store to help furnish toys to children who might not receive anything otherwise. Lula Belle Puckett is the present coordinator, and several volunteers donate their time helping out. Churches, businesses, and other organizations make donations through the year to help with expenses.

On what is now called Jefferson Street was White's Opera House. It sat on the northwest corner across the street from the Clinton Hardware Store. Jacob White and T. W. Ashley built it in 1880 as partners. The opera house was on the second floor, while Ashley's Dry Goods Store was on the bottom. The building burned in 1911.

Today the empty lot on the corner of Jefferson and West Clay Streets and Creative Printing, next door, sit on the site of the opera house. The printing company is owned and operated by Jeff Breedlove. Customers can have stationery, business cards, envelopes, letterheads, and much more printed here.

The west side of the courthouse square is also home to M&J Angel House, a gift shop that includes flower arrangements, ceramic gifts, candles, and Willow Tree Angels. The Clinton City Hall is a couple of doors down, and one can find the Hickman County Extension Service in the last building on the square.

In 1940, the Jackson Poultry House was located on Depot Street; the building just burned in 2009. The business sold different breeds of chickens and bought eggs from its patrons. Seated is Huey Jackson with Glyn Jackson, his son, and Doris Jackson, his daughter-in-law. (Courtesy of Norma Dean Beadles.)

Grogan's Bar B Que is housed on the corner of Highways 51 and 58. Red and Alene Grogan own and operate the business. They sell barbeque by the pound and also have buffet-type plate lunches seven days a week, as well as serving breakfast. One can buy drinks, chips, cigarettes, gas, and ice cream. This, at one time, was Weatherford's Service Station.

This building was the home of the *Hickman County Gazette* for several years. Ed B. Walker began publication of the *Twice-A-Week-Gazette* in 1901, later to become the *Hickman County Gazette*. At Walker's death in 1914, his widow ran the *Gazette* until 1923, when it was sold to A. E. Stein. Stein printed the paper until selling in 1932 to Earl Ward Jr., who after only two years sold to Harry Lee Waterfield. This building was destroyed by high winds in 2007. Only the Clinton Bank building is left today. The *Gazette* moved to the Yates Building. Gaye Bencini is the news editor and Nancy Evans is the office manager.

In 1925, Bynum Jackson bought the McLemore Insurance Agency and established it as Jackson Insurance Agency. When Jackson died, his son-in-law, Jimmy Weatherford, became the field representative and Mary Nell Jackson Weatherford was the office manager. The agency moved to the north side of East Clay Street, where this picture was taken. The men are, from left to right, unidentified, Jackson, unidentified, and Jimmy Weatherford. Later the agency moved to the south side of East Clay Street next to the *Hickman County Gazette* office. (Courtesy of Annell Orlando.)

Edward Thomas came to Clinton in 1949. He set up a stand in Parker's Restaurant, making watch repairs. In July 1950, he opened his jewelry store first on Jefferson Street (west side of courthouse square), and in 1951, he located his business on East Clay Street next to Jackson Insurance Agency.

On the north corner of Highway 51 and East Clay Street was Brummal Brothers Grocery. This picture is of the interior of Brummal Brothers Grocery with owners and customers. Pictured from left to right are Quigley Brummal, Jimmy Bowden, Clarence Heaslet, Warren Brummal, and Stumpy Jordan. Not only could customers eat at the lunch counter, but they could buy from the large assortment of groceries also.

A couple of doors down from Brummal Brothers was the W. C. Hutcherson and Company Dry Goods Store. The business was started in 1915 and was housed on the east side of the courthouse square. In this picture, one can see the ritzy interior of the store built in 1923. This building was one of the first businesses in the county to have running water, steam heat, and inside toilets. Later this store was bought by Tommy Williams and was in business for several years. The building was torn down in 2003 and is now the home of Jackson Purchase ACA.

The Strand Theatre was next door to Hutcherson's. Rodolph and Becky Bryan operated it from 1945 until 1964. The theater opened in 1936 and was one of a chain of theaters operated in West Kentucky, Tennessee, Arkansas, and Mississippi. Clinton was without a "picture show" for about 10 to 12 years before the Strand opened again in 1945. Many children in this area spent Saturday afternoon at the movies eating popcorn and drinking Coca-cola. Today this building has also been demolished and is part of the Jackson Purchase ACA Building lot.

This is the new Jackson Purchase ACA Building being built in the summer of 2009. ACA has moved from the Yates Building. These lots have seen many stores in years gone by. There was Paddy's Corner, the Greenhouse, Brummal Brothers, Hutcherson's, Williams Dry Goods, the Johnson Poolhall, and the law offices of Roberts, Bugg, and Morris. The stores of yesteryear are all gone now, either having been torn down or burned.

Robert Johnson (left) and Walter Wayne Weatherford can be seen here in front of Weatherford's Service Station in 1971. The station was located on the corner of Highways 51 and 58. Weatherford ran the station until the summer of 1981, when it was closed.

Above is the Clinton Post Office in 1953. This building was occupied in 1942, but the post office had been in several other buildings before this one. Pictured from left to right are Wood Jones, Will Nall, Speight Brazzell, Jewell Via, Ben Hales Jr., Henry Brazzell Jr., Harry "Pete" Halterman, postmistress Genia Hilliard, Georgia Via, Harold "Sleepy" Poole, Julius Reese, Henry Brazzell Sr., R. F. Claud Sr., Butler Ringo, Joe Ward, and J. R. Brazzell. The picture below is the Clinton Post Office today.

The first courthouse in Clinton was built of logs in 1829. It served the county until 1832, when a new building was erected. It was made of brick and was two stories high, with the courtroom below and three jury rooms on the second floor. When it was completed, it was the only brick house in Kentucky west of the Tennessee River. It served the people of Hickman County until 1883, when it was razed and the one in the picture was built.

Ruby Faye's Restaurant, located on Highway 51 South one-half mile from Clinton, was opened in 2008 by owners and operators Gordon and Ruth Ann Samples and Ken and Ann Jewell. They serve an assortment of plate lunches, sandwiches, wraps, and salads. They also have barbeque by the pound, and they will cater meals if needed. The restaurant was named for Gordon's mother, Ruby Samples, who was a beloved schoolteacher in the county. Bob Samples, Gordon's father, makes the blackberry cobbler, one of the desserts available. The homemade ice cream and peanut butter pie are delicious.

Piper's Drive Inn was the local hangout for all the kids, especially the teenagers, in the 1950s and 1960s. It was located on Highway 51 south of Clinton. One could eat at the counter or in booths or sit in the car and have curb service. Owned and operated by Jimmy and Mable Piper, it was the first place teens went on a Friday or Saturday night. The food was delicious and the company great. (Courtesy of Mabel Piper.)

# Two

# CHURCHES
## HOUSES OF WORSHIP

Mount Pleasant United Methodist Church was the first church built in Hickman County. In 1823, "a round-pole cabin" with dirt floors and an open fireplace was erected for a place of worship. Pastor Abram Long was the first to have an organized church held at Mount Pleasant. There have been a total of six buildings built on this same site for a church building. One was destroyed by a tornado in 1918, and another burned in 1935. The church pictured was erected in 1936 and was enlarged in 1955 and 1979. In 2001, an activity building was begun and completed in 2004.

First Assembly of God Church was started in 1920. The first meetings were held in a large tent. During a revival that lasted eight weeks, many people received the baptism in the Holy Spirit. After the meeting, the church rented several places to have Sunday services until Emma Cooper bought a lot in 1942 and deeded the lot to the church. A brick building was built and used as the church until 1992, when the church body built a new building on Highway 51 North.

The Boaz Chapel Primitive Church is located about 2 miles east of Fulton on the Tennessee and Kentucky State Line Road and Highway 1218 in Hickman County. Grove Church started meeting with the congregation at Boaz Chapel. In 1889, Thomas Boaz deeded some acreage to build the present-day church building. The church hitching ground was across the road from the church in Tennessee.

First Baptist Church, Clinton, Ky.

1910

In December 1833, the Clinton Baptist Church of Jesus Christ was organized with Elder J. P. Edwards as the first pastor. In the latter part of 1851, Clinton Baptist Church bought a lot where Williams Hardware was and erected a story-and-a-half wooden building. The church used the bottom floor for services while the Masonic Lodge occupied the second floor. In 1890, when this building could no longer be used or improved, the church erected a house of worship on a donated lot on the southeast corner of the courthouse square. This is the church pictured in the above photograph. Below is the First Baptist Church today, built in 1964. A gymnasium has been added, and a remodeling phase began in 2003.

Mount Moriah Missionary Baptist Church was organized in 1875. The first records show that a building was erected in 1889. In 1904, the community bought a bell to be used for the announcement of church services or for an emergency. This same bell is now sitting on the front lawn of the present-day church. The 1889 church was destroyed by a heavy windstorm in 1942. A brick building was built mostly with donated labor. This is the present-day building; the pioneering founders would be proud of the devotion the members have today.

Located on Highway 1529 about three-fourths of a mile off Highway 51 East is the New Hope Missionary Baptist Church. It was organized in 1842 with 50 members out of First Baptist Church of Clinton. There have been at least four other Baptist churches organized out of New Hope Church. These are Mount Moriah, New Bethel, Mount Carmel, and Crutchfield Baptist Church. In the past several years, there has been a revival in this church and its congregation has grown. Br. Randy McClure is the pastor.

As shown in the above picture, the first Mount Sinai Missionary Baptist Church was built in 1881. For many years, the congregation met in this tiny clapboard building. Its cornerstone still exists today, as it was cemented into the new building. The worshippers met in the first building until the 1950s; it had become so ramshackle, it could no longer be used. They then moved into an abandoned clapboard one-room school building. This building was not much better than the old one. So in 1975, the old church was torn down and a new one was built.

In December 1876, Ezkiel and Louise Rambo deeded land to the Pleasant Valley Baptist Church. There have been three church buildings located on this site. The present brick building was erected in 1970. In 2003, a fellowship hall was built. Today Rev. Tim Stinson is pastor.

Springhill Baptist Church was formed in 1842. It was first called Cypress Baptist Church and was located a few miles east of the present site. The first church building was destroyed by fire about 1900, but the congregation rebuilt the church house in 1901 on the present site. A two-story Sunday school room annex was built onto the back of the church in 1948. In 1989, a fellowship hall was added and, in 1992, a baptistery.

In 1894, in a missionary tent of the West Kentucky Baptist Association, individuals of Oakton gathered to worship. At the end of the service, the congregation decided to organize a Baptist church. On January 12, 1895, Oakton Baptist Church held its first meeting. A new building had been built, and the pulpit of that church is still being used today at the church building constructed in 1969. Since then, the church members have added Sunday school rooms, a fellowship hall, a kitchen, and a playground. Br. Ricky Harrison is pastor.

The Clinton Primitive Baptist Church building was completed in 1995. It is located on Circle Road, south of Clinton off of Highway 51. Eddie Hicks is the pastor today.

The Beulah Baptist Church was first called the United Baptist Church of Christ at Pleasant Ridge. This church was organized in 1863 and was used until 1877, when a group of men decided to build a better church building. They built the new church one-half mile west of the old one. It remains there today, now on Highway 307. In 1976, a new auditorium was built. Since then, a recreation building has been constructed along with a carport for the buses. Brother Allred is minister today.

Columbus Baptist Church was officially organized in 1842, but some other church records mention an "Iron Bank Baptist Church" as far back as 1810. Since Columbus was called Iron Banks at one time, several people think these two churches are one and the same. The flood of 1927 destroyed all of the present-day church records. The last Sunday school held under the hill was in December 1927. After that, the American Red Cross moved the building up the hill; the building was restored and is being used today.

Green Valley Baptist Church is located on Blair Street in Clinton. In 1869, Marion Ray and John Moore deeded a plot of land to the church and a box building was raised. Under the guidance of the Reverends Bill Johnson, Charles Williams, Jacke Johnson, and Alex Brevoid, Green Valley Baptist Church was organized. In 1919, a new building was erected, and after 47 years of worship in this building, the funds were raised to build a new church building. In 1966, one was erected, and today Br. Eugene McDonald leads this congregation.

Moscow Baptist Church was organized in 1892, and a sanctuary was constructed in 1894. In 1952, the church building was remodeled and two Sunday school rooms were added. A full-time pastor was obtained in 1954 when the church called Rev. Billy Moreland. In 1962, further remodeling was done with a baptistery added. Donald Gibson was the first person to be baptized in the new baptistery. A dredge ditch had been used before to baptize earlier converts.

The above picture is a view of the old Mount Gilead Missionary Baptist Church Building. It was erected in 1873 under the hill in Columbus. During the flood of 1927, the building was moved up the hill and used until June 1997, when it was destroyed by fire. The picture below is the new church building erected in 1998–1999. It was dedicated on February 22, 1999.

In the year 1913, Obion Church was organized. Plans were made to build a church near Obion Creek in the Springhill community. The church was destroyed by fire, but the congregation decided to rebuild. Many seasons of high water caused the members to decide to move the church. Jerry R. Johnson donated land for the church. In 1971, Bob Brown sold the old Kane School to the congregation, and they renovated it to be their new church building. So the New Obion Missionary Baptist Church was born and sits on Kane Street in Clinton today.

Second Baptist Church was started through the mission affiliated with what is now Mid-Continent Baptist College. Some members who attended the mission left to help organize Second Baptist Church. First Baptist Church helped by giving the land where the building was erected in 1954. In 2009, the members had started to add to the building when a fire struck and destroyed not only the new building but the old one as well. The members are now meeting at the First Christian Church until they determine where they will build again. Br. Larry Fraser is the pastor.

New Harmony Baptist Church is located on Highway 123 North about 5 miles from Clinton. In the past several years, this country church has added twice onto the sanctuary, added a fellowship hall and playground, and blacktopped and added to the parking lot. For the past 15 or so years, Br. David Gossum has pastored this congregation.

There is very little known about the early history of New Bethel Baptist Church. It sits on a lot about 2 miles south of the Fulgham community on Highway 307. There is a deed that states Silas Clark gave the land for the church to be built in 1893. Rev. Ronald Cruse is the pastor today.

The newest church to be formed in Hickman County is the Hope Community Church. Pastor Ken Jewell and his congregation hold services at the church building located on James Phillips Drive. This group first started meeting in Ruby Faye's Restaurant and grew until they needed to find other accommodations. The building they are in now once housed the Assembly of God Church. They serve coffee and doughnuts on Sunday morning before worship. Also, they have met several times at Columbus-Belmont Park for worship and a meal that follows.

The First Christian Church was organized in 1876. A frame building was built and used until 1896, when it was destroyed by fire. The members decided to rebuild on the same spot, and a new brick building was finished in 1899. This building served the members of First Christian Church until late in 2008, when the membership was reduced to a very few people. Br. Bob Roberts is the pastor. Clinton Second Baptist Church has been allowed to use the facilities for their church service since the fire destroyed that church.

The First United Methodist Church, in 1857, built a log structure to be used by the congregation as a church home until 1876, when this property was transferred to the Presbyterian church and the lot was bought where the present-day church is standing. The brick church was built and has been in use until recently with an addition to the building in 1906. Several renovations have been completed, and the Young Center—used by the community as well as the church for weddings, receptions, reunions, and so forth—was built alongside the church. Rev. Aaron Dowdy is the present minister.

Harmony Methodist Church came into existence in about 1849. This church was located in the southwest part of Hickman County next to the Fulton County line. There have been three church buildings, with the present one built in 1912. The church was closed several years ago, but the Kentucky Heritage Commission designated Harmony Methodist Church a Kentucky landmark.

Columbus Methodist Church was organized in 1879, and the church building was finished and used until the 1927 flood of Columbus. During the flood, the building was flooded, and as the picture to the right shows, the building was moved to the top of the hill at the present site of the church. Below is the same building, which is being used today by a small but active congregation, renamed the Columbus Community River Mission Church.

In 1894, the community banded together and built a brush arbor with a Reverend Fold and a Reverend Hardin doing the preaching. As a result of that revival, Mount Vernon Methodist Church came into existence. The first site for the church adjoined the Judge Brummal farm. In 1928, the church building was moved to a site on Highway 51 South. The membership slowly decreased, and the church was finally closed. The building was torn away and the land sold.

New Chapel Methodist Church was one of the oldest churches in the county. Some of the church records dated back to 1837 when Matilda Vaughan took her marriage vows. In 1873, J. M. Caldwell gave an acre of land to be used as the site for a new church building. The New Chapel Church was located on State Route 1540, and the cemetery property adjoined the property of the church. The church is now closed, and the building has been destroyed. Some of the older church members are still being buried in the cemetery.

The Oakton Methodist Church was started in 1893, but before the church building was finished, it was destroyed by a tornado. The members rebuilt the church and used it until 1953, when a fire completely destroyed the building. The congregation rebuilt in the spring of 1954. Today there is a very small group of dedicated people who continue to worship at the church.

In August 1871, John Bryars and John Utterback donated 2 acres of land where Oakwood Methodist Church was built. The cemetery acreage was also sold to the trustees for $150. The church at this time was located in the cemetery. In 1890, a tornado badly damaged the clapboard church and the members made plans to rebuild. In 1895, a brick building was erected across the road from the old church site. In May 1917, Oakwood Church was sitting in the direct path of another tornado and was completely destroyed. The church building that is still being used today was built in 1918. Rev. Aaron Dowdy is the pastor.

First called "The Meeting House" as early as 1837, Salem United Methodist Church was organized and a church building erected in 1874. The first log church stood south of the old frame church and across the road from where the brick building is now standing. The site of the old church on the west side of the road has become a cemetery. This picture is of the brick building constructed in 1940 and used until 2006, when the church closed its doors. The building is now for sale.

This is the third church building that housed the membership of the Shiloh Methodist Church. The first building, made of logs, sat across the road from the present-day building on an acre of land donated by Michael Ward in 1835. The site of the old church is now in the Shiloh Cemetery. In 1871, a frame clapboard structure was built across the road on land deeded by Frank Bone. This was used until the present brick building was built in 1891. In 2008, a Sunday school room was renovated into a kitchen and dining area for members to use. The small membership of devoted individuals is keeping the doors of Shiloh Methodist Church open to anyone who would like to attend.

The Zion Methodist Church near Columbus was formed in 1881. H. B. French donated the land on the Columbus-Oakton Highway. Some of the charter members were H. B. French, R. T. Samuel, and C. E. Bussey. In 1942, the first building burned and was replaced by a brick structure. The church has been abandoned for several years.

Today Wesley Methodist Church can be found on Highway 1529 west off of Highway 307 South. Mark Hardin is said to have donated the land for the first church, made of logs. Around 1883, that church burned, but the congregation rebuilt quickly and the building was in use until the 1930s. It was decided that the building was no longer functional and a new structure was erected. This is the building being used today with a few remodeling features made during the past years.

Greenwood Christian Church was located at the intersection of the old Union City Road and "Upper Bottom" Road on the Mobile and Ohio Railroad (M&O) at what is called Greenwood Crossing. It was built around 1877 and was destroyed by fire about 1920. Some of the families worshipping there were the Caldwells, Deweeses, Jordans, Mosiers, Craigs, Benthals, and Utterbacks.

The only Cumberland Presbyterian Church in Hickman County is known as Mount Zion. It is located in the southeast part of the county. It was formed in 1842 on land donated by James McAlister. There have been three buildings the congregation has worshipped in. The first was a log structure used until 1886, when a new frame building was constructed. The present-day church was dedicated in 1949.

The Moores Chapel AME Church can be found on the corner of Depot and Angular Streets.

In 1882, W. A. Gibson gathered together some old members of the Gilgal Church, baptized some, and constituted the church called Webb's Chapel Church of Christ. The church can be found on State Route 1772 about 3 miles from Arlington.

St. Denis Catholic Church can be found on State Route 1748 in the northeastern part of Hickman County . Pictured is the facility built in 1914 on land donated by Mr. and Mrs. L. W. Ellegood. A new brick church building, constructed in 1981, will seat 300 people and is being used today.

After several services were held in the Hickman County Recreation Center, it was decided that a Catholic parish would be started in Clinton. Thus the Church of St. Jude was established in 1982. A church building was erected and is located on Highway 58 one block from Highway 51 South.

Jackson Chapel Church is located on State Route 944 in the southeastern part of the county. It is one of the oldest churches in the county, having been formed in 1825. The first building was of logs and was used until 1897, when the second building was erected. In 1951, the present church was built, and since that time, a Sunday school area has been added. Jackson Chapel is well known for its ice cream socials during the summer months.

This is an image of the old Rock Springs Primitive Baptist Church, which was located in the southern part of the county along what is now Highway 51.

The Meeting Room is located on Highway 123 north near Columbus Road. The breaking of bread is on Sunday at 11:00 a.m. with Bible study Sunday and Wednesday nights.

# *Three*

# COMMUNITIES
## FROM BEULAH TO BOAZ CHAPEL,
## WOLF ISLAND TO ST. DENNIS,
## AND ALL IN BETWEEN

Wolf Island is the property of Kentucky and Hickman County, but it is actually across the Mississippi River from both. It does, however, touch Missouri. A channel of the river once ran between the north bank of the island and the Missouri shore. But since the 1927 flood, the river has gradually shifted its channel to the Kentucky side. John H. Irby, the island's oldest inhabitant, and his family are shown on the steps of their house on Wolf Island. The picture, taken about 1928, shows, from left to right, (first row) John Jr. and Marie Irby; (second row) Ellen, Cora, and John Irby. This house was the last house to stand on the island. (Courtesy of Kay Cooper.)

Near the Beulah community, in the northeastern part of Hickman County, one can find one of the last undisturbed natural cypress swamps, known as Murphy's Pond. It is reached from Highway 1748 near Beulah on Murphy's Pond Road. Since 1975, Murray State University has owned the pond and uses it as an outdoor classroom. Visitors can enjoy native trees and wildflowers from a wooden walkway that leads through part of the 28-acre pond. Deer, birds, raccoons, opossums, fox, and other wildlife can be seen in abundance. Also the pond is well known for its large snake population.

Pictured to the left is the building that was home to the store known as "Rule Shack." It was located on the Graves-Hickman County line on Highway 1686 and was owned first by John Rule and then by Clois Wilson. It was a small, one-room country store selling soft drinks, candy, and general merchandise but, most of all, supplying a place for the half-dozen or so "regulars" who gathered to discuss the latest topics.

In 1941, Loyd Courtney bought the old Beulah Baptist Church building and moved his store into it. This is a picture of Loyd Courtney and Company General Merchandise that was located on the corner of Highway 307 and 1748. After operating the store for several years, Courtney leased it to Williard Wilson, and he operated it until it burned in the 1970s.

The only store known to be in the Croley community was Weatherford's Grocery. Around 1950, Morris Weatherford purchased the grocery from his parents, William and Lillian Weatherford. He sold general merchandise, gas, light hardware, and feed. In 1971, the building was torn down and a new one erected. Maurice later sold the store to Ron Cooley, who sold it to Jim Aldridge.

Marvin Burkett is shown in his general store in the Fulgham community. It was located on the southwest corner at the four-way stop. He bought the store from Presley Vaughan and operated it until he retired in 1951. He also operated a "peddlers wagon" from the store. It carried grocery staples and penny candy to customers in the community. The customers did not always have cash, so they paid with eggs, cream, chickens, or whatever they had to trade. There is no longer a store building on that corner. (Courtesy of Robert Burkett.)

The A&W Grocery located also in Fulgham has been one of the longest operated grocery stores in the county. Thomas Wilkins and S. R. Armbruster Jr. first operated it and then sold the business to Hazel and Herschel Whitlock around 1954. Hazel sold the store to Robert Burkett and his son Jeff, who ran the store for a couple of years. The store has been closed in the past year, and now Dean Sullenger owns the property and will use the store building for a shop.

This picture shows a *c.* 1900 traveling sawmill. It would chug from one place to another and set up shop where it was needed. The steam-powered sawmill had a wood-fired boiler. Iron castings and a wooden cradle are other features of the sawmill. Dave Humphreys, father of W. W. Humphreys of the Fulgham community, is second from right sitting on a log.

The Oakton community is located in the western part of Hickman County. The Mobile & Ohio (M&O) Railroad, later known as the Gulf, Mobile, & Ohio (GM&O) Railroad, was completed around 1858, and a depot was built in Oakton with Judge Naylor as the depot agent. It was one of the most popular places in town. People came to ship their crops, such as wheat, corn, and cotton. Also the train brought bags of mail for the people of Oakton and the surrounding area. The passenger service was discontinued in 1953, and the line was completely abandoned in 1978.

Pictured here are, from left to right, Will Salmon, George Sweezy, Dan Shaw, and Nick Fowlkes as they unload a wagon of corn onto a car of the M&O Railroad at the Oakton Depot.

This is a train wreck that happened in 1930 in Oakton. Several cars were derailed, and Leon Parr, a hobo, was killed.

This is the Mills residence in Oakton around the dawn of the 20th century. Pictured from left to right are Agnes, Mack, Kittie, and Elbert Mills. This home burned in 1923 and stood where the Lelia Moser home now stands.

This building was used for the Oakton Post Office after about 1930 until it closed on March 23, 1989. Sue Brummal was the postmistress when it closed. It is believed to have been the office of Dr. J. R. Wrather around 1900.

Elbert Mills is sitting on the right, and the man on the left is unidentified. They are on the porch of the Utterback Store located in Oakton. It was one of the very early stores and was owned by George Utterback. This building burned in 1912, and the store was opened in another building. The bank building was then built on this lot.

Claud "Dock" Williams (left) and Emmett Burcham are seen in Dock's general store in Oakton. Dock came back to Oakton in 1919 after serving in World War I and clerked in Utterback's Store for a while. Later he opened his own store and sold general store merchandise to the Oakton community for 49 years. He retired in 1968 and was known throughout Oakton as "Mr. Penny Candy Man" because of the candy he sold and gave to all of the children in the community. (Courtesy of Estelle Morris.)

Dave Craddock established a canning factory in Oakton in 1913. It manufactured canned goods such as tomatoes. He closed the factory in 1932.

This is a label from a can of tomatoes that was canned at the Oakton Canning Factory.

Earnest Kelly was the town's barber for 50 years. He began barbering in 1921 and retired in 1971. This building was the home of Kelly's shop. Electricity did not come to Oakton until 1939, so for 18 years, he used hand clippers to cut hair. The haircuts cost all of a quarter, and some of his customers would charge them until the crops were made and then come by and settle their account.

This picture is of the Oakton Bank Building in 1989. Ruben Griffey and Henry Alexander served as cashiers of the bank. The Oakton Bank ceased to exist in 1933 when Clinton Bank absorbed their business.

In 1912, when the Missouri levee was built, it doomed some of the outlying homes and farms around the Oakton community. These pictures show houses, located in the Oakton "bottoms," that were affected by the flood of 1913. Even though the houses were built on stilts, the floodwaters rose so high at times that the houses and other outbuildings were flooded to the rooftops. Gradually, after being flooded several times, the families decided to move to higher ground.

As the caption says, this is a bird's-eye view of the city of old Columbus "under the hill." This picture was taken before 1927. Columbus was located on the banks of the mighty Mississippi River. In 1927, there was a flood and the river literally engulfed the town. Several of the buildings were moved "up the hill" and the others were lost to the river. Columbus is often called "the city that should have been."

This street scene of old Columbus shows the old Columbus School Building, in the right foreground, with the clock tower. This picture, taken in 1913, shows on the left the levee that was to protect the buildings from the floodwaters. The City Council House is next to the school with Gib and Sally Pollock Lee's home in the foreground. Laverne Snell had drilled the students so thoroughly that they were able to move up onto the levee before the raging water rushed into the building 4 feet deep.

This is a picture of old Columbus in 1900. The buildings on the right side of Kentucky Street, in the foreground, for the most part caved into the Mississippi River during the flood of 1927. The city was moved one-half mile eastward and built upon a high bluff by the American Red Cross after the flooding.

In 1871, the St. Louis and Iron Mountain Railroad was built into Belmont, Missouri, which lies just opposite of Columbus. A transfer ferryboat was established to carry the train's cars, engines, and caboose across the river to Columbus. This picture shows the ferry carrying a railroad steam engine across the river. The St. Louis, Iron Mountain, and Southern Railroad discontinued service to old Columbus in 1911.

This is an 1883 picture of the old *St. Louis* transfer ferry. Capt. L. T. Bradley is on the upper deck in front of the pilothouse. Charles E. Medley is behind the coal car. Henry Gail is in the group on deck. Julius Hough is the engineer, and Sidney Gail is the fireman.

The Fourth of July celebration in old Columbus was a tradition that was started as early as 1832. This is the parade in 1908. Hundreds of people from miles away would flock to Columbus to enjoy the observance of this holiday.

This is a float entered in a parade by Summers Drug Store. In the background, one can see a few of the buildings that housed businesses in old Columbus. The date of this picture is unknown.

In 1927, the floodwaters rose, the levees began to break, and the town of old Columbus was about to succumb to the mighty river. Looking to the north, one will see Main Street in old Columbus. The brick building on the right is the bank, and the next one is Morrison Grocery.

This is the old Columbus School building that was located "under the hill" and was destroyed by the flood in 1927. The clock in the tower was saved and was installed in the new school building on top of the hill. After the Columbus School was consolidated with Clinton, the building was abandoned and torn down. The clock was removed and placed on the top of the water tower in new Columbus and is still there today, as shown in the picture below.

This picture, taken in the 1880s, shows a store (possibly a drugstore) that sat on Roan Street in old Columbus. On the back, it has stamped "H. R. Lower, Druggist, Columbus, Kentucky." Later on, this was also the post office of old Columbus.

Winn House Moving Company of Nashville and Clarksville, Tennessee, helped to move the city, or what was left of it, to the bluff. This is the home of Brown Marre after it was moved to its place in new Columbus. It was the first building to be moved up the hill.

These are some of the men who worked for Winn House Moving Company. Below is a tractor and truck used in moving the buildings. In the background can be seen a house they are pulling up the bluff.

This picture shows some of the houses that had been moved to the bluff from old Columbus in 1928. The street is Hoover Parkway, and the houses on the left belonged to ? Carter, George Avey, Luther Morrison, Luther Sanders, Carrie Griggs, and Sam Byassee. Those who lived on the right were the Aveys, Billy Roberts, ? Summers, Bessie Kerr, and ? Moss.

Since the old Columbus School was destroyed in the flood, a new one was built on top of the bluff. This is the new Columbus School when finished. The building was used until the school was consolidated with Clinton. Today the building is gone, but the memories live on.

The Red Cross was instrumental in forming the city of new Columbus. These are pictures of the camp established by Marion Rust, representative of the Red Cross. It provided food, shelter, medicine, and other necessities for the refugees of Columbus. Below, from left to right, are Lida Glass, R. C. Summers, Mont Medley, Frank Wright, Marion Rust, Laverne Snell, and three unidentified.

Morrison Grocery was first known as Morrison and Fisher Store when the town was under the hill. Luther Morrison and his partner, Mr. Fisher, owned the store that was destroyed in the flood of 1927. The above picture is of the interior of Morrison Grocery, which was built when Columbus was moved to the top of the hill and owned by Luther Morrison and then his son and daughter-in-law, "Big" Jimmy and Mildred Morrison. The picture below is of the store in the 1970s. The store burned in 1980.

Today Columbus is known for the Columbus-Belmont State Park. Manager Cindy Lynch has renovated the park since taking office and made it an enjoyable place to picnic, hike, or just look at nature. The park has the Civil War Museum, a miniature golf course, playground equipment, a food bar, and several scenic overlooks. The Civil War trenches and fortifications are extremely interesting to see.

The Columbus Belmont Battlefield Park Association was incorporated in 1928. There were several fund-raising drives. One is shown in this picture taken about 1933. Marion Rust was the driving force to obtain the acres for the park. He oversaw the Civilian Conservation Corps (CCC) camp boys who worked from 1934 to 1937 to build the park. The CCC camp was located at what is now the park camping area.

On the steps of the Moscow Bank that opened in 1904 were some of the town's leading citizens. From left to right are Leslie Robertson, depot agent; Fred Brock Sr., cashier; Bud Kimbro, mail carrier; and Ira Little, a merchant. The Woodmen of the World, Modern Woodmen of America, and the Masonic Lodge held their meetings on the second floor of the bank. The bank closed in the early 1920s.

This is a picture of a couple of wagons loaded with logs ready to go to a sawmill. The wagons were called "dog wagons" and were pulled by four or five head of mules. The teamster rode in a saddle on the back of one of the mules and held lines to the leader that were hooked to the end of the wagon tongue. Evidently, they had arrived at the railroad yard since, in the background, one can see cars on the railroad track. The teamsters are unidentified.

Moscow at one time was a growing and prosperous town. Lane and Roberts General Merchandise store was just one of several businesses in Moscow. Vester Roberts and B. F. Lane were the owners and operators. Customers could buy or trade for just about anything they were in need of. Also around 1908, schoolchildren could even buy their standard textbook from the store. Identified persons in the first row are Jim Flatt (far left), ? Kyles (second from the left), John Sexton (seventh from the left), and Rev. R. E. Brassfield (far right).

This is a picture of the old Moscow ferry as it was crossing the Bayou de Chien. Notice the lady with the gun.

These houses were located in the Moscow community. The above picture is of the Little family's home, and below is that of the Ramer family. The Little family owned the J. T. Little General Store during the first part of the 1900s. Grace Ramer was a schoolteacher, while Nannu Kate Ramer was an operator for the telephone switchboard.

This is a picture of what was once Pharis Grocery in the Shiloh community. Bill and Maxie Pharis operated it for several years. Shown is the daughter of Bill Pharis, Sophia Pharis. T. L. Ezell was the owner before the Pharis family bought it. It was called the New Cypress Store or just Cypress Store. The store stocked just about anything customers could want: huge barrels with nails, bolts, hammers, sacks of flour and meal, beautiful bolts of colored material and all the sewing notions to go with it, dishes, overalls, work jackets and shirts, canned goods, glass jars of dried fruit, barrels of sugar, and of course the candy and chewing gum. The store has been closed for several years, and the building has been torn down. (Courtesy of Sophia Pharis Barclay.)

The Springhill community had its own store—the Featherstone Grocery. Earl and Mae Featherstone owned and operated this country store that they began about 1923. The store above housed the post office, an ice cream parlor with a soda fountain, and the grocery. It burned about 1965. Earlier T. L. Ezell ran a peddler's wagon from the store.

This is the second building to house the Featherstone Grocery. Earl and Mae built this block building when the first store burned. It is now closed, and the building has been abandoned.

This is a picture of Eugene Henley and his crew ready to start wheat threshing in the Springhill community. As the thresher moved through the field, the teams of horses, pulling wagons, would carry the wheat to the mill or wherever the farmer would have it placed.

The Springhill Courthouse has seen better days. But in years past, this small white frame building was the voting precinct for over 90 years. In the very early days of the community, it served as a magistrate's court and some civil and "kangaroo" trials were held here; hence it was nicknamed "the courthouse."

In 1918, Wilma Brummal took this photograph of four teams of mules and a wagon hauling the base to the large marker in the center of the cemetery. This cemetery, known as the Johnson Cemetery, is located near Springhill. The marker was brought on a flat car after being shipped here from France. The cemetery is located north of the community and is the final resting place of several of the African American families who lived nearby, as well as the white community. (Courtesy of Jim and Sue Brummal.)

Around 1890, Sam Grogan Sr. had a sawmill in Hickman County. No one seems to know just where it was located. Standing from left to right are Otis Grogan, unidentified, Lynn Ingram, unidentified, Sam Grogan Jr., two unidentified, and John Pickard. Standing under the shed in back of the fourth man from the left is Sam Grogan Sr. He can hardly be seen.

FRED HUDSON'S GROCERY — Highway 51

Fred Hudson owned and operated Hudson's Grocery. It was located on Highway 51 south of Clinton. He sold staple and fancy groceries, gas, oil, cold drinks, and other items customers needed. The house next to the store building was his residence. The store has been gone for several years, but the house is still being used as a residence.

Nicky's Bar-B-Que, located on Highway 51 North, is owned and operated by Nicky McClanahan. Customers can dine on sandwiches or plate lunches or buy barbeque by the pound. Nicky also caters for different occasions and has a trailer that travels to auctions, where he sells sandwiches, cold drinks, potato chips, and candy. Before Nicky went into business, Woodye Smith (above) was the operator of Woodye's Bar-B-Que for several years in the same location. In 1974, Woodye was ready to retire and Nicky went into business. Woodye stayed with Nicky for about a year, teaching him how to cook on the "pit." (Both courtesy of Sylvia Ward.)

A wagon and horse was about the only transportation one had in 1928 on Wolf Island. Here in the wagon from left to right are John Irby Jr., Vernon Holder (seated), and Gene Holder. On the ground, Sonny Irby is holding Kay Irby. The only other way to travel was by foot or by boat. (Courtesy of Kay Cooper.)

At the back of the Irby house was the pump for getting water. John Irby is using the handle to pump water into the trough that ran to the barrel or bucket to fill. One can see the stack of wood in the background. This was used to cook with and, in the winter, to warm the house. (Courtesy of Kay Cooper.)

This is a picture of Montra Allen, a schoolteacher at the Wolf Island School. She would board with the Irbys when she was teaching during the week. On weekends or holidays, one of the men would take her across the Mississippi River to Columbus, where someone would meet her. On Sunday afternoon, they would retrace their steps and she would be back to teach on Monday morning. (Courtesy of Kay Cooper.)

*Four*

# ACTIVITIES
## EVENTS, ADVENTURES,
## AND EXPERIENCES

Oakton High School opened in 1924 with grades 1 through 12. These are the Oakton 1932 basketball champions. From left to right are June Kimble, Velma Stephens, Rema O'Bryant, Lottie King, Christine McBride (seated), Dentis McDaniel (coach and principal), Frances Berry, Hattie Lee Taylor, and Pearl Ferguson. (Courtesy of Ruth Curlin.)

In 1971, the residents of Hickman County observed their sesquicentennial celebration. Several events took place during the week. One of the events held was a parade through downtown Clinton. The picture on the left shows one of the entries was an old steam engine. The one below is an early mode of transportation—the stagecoach being pulled by mules.

Several of the inhabitants of Hickman County joined in the fun by dressing as some of the pioneers would have 150 years ago. Pictured here from left to right are Hilda Brazzell, Margaret Campbell, and Imogene Lemond.

This Model T car was cruising along in the parade.

Porter's Tuffs baseball team consisted, from left to right, of the following: (first row) Phil Porter, Lewis Jewell, Bill Porter, and George Utterback; (second row) Roy Tooms, ? Farmer, Woodson Earle, Fred Elliott, ? Underwood, Warren Brummal, and Joe Johnson.

This is the Marvin College baseball team about 1916–1917. They were, from left to right, (first row) unidentified and Phil Porter; (second row) Roy Tooms, Charles Carman, and Lloyd Carter; (third row) Joe Johnson, ? McAlister, ? Moore, unidentified, Bob Humphreys, and ? Goddard.

The Clinton Dixie League team were the league champions with a record of 22 wins and 2 losses. Members of the team were, from left to right, (first row) Jim Morrison, James Lamkins, Ray Hopper, Jerry Featherstone, John Muscovalley, Bill Prince, and James Mathis; (second row) Obert Bushart (manager), Bob Conn, Jerry Bohn, Joe Lamkins, June Hicks, Stan Griffin, and W. R. Trimble. Four members of the team were absent when the picture was made—Bill Kaler, Curtis Wilson, Walter Canty, and Jerry Bone.

The seven-man squad of the 1925 Clinton High School basketball team was the first winning basketball team that can be remembered. Members are, from left to right, Zearl Davis, Willis Hilliard, Finley Rennick, Harry Brinkley, Vester Jackson, Henry Norman "Adam" Weatherford, and Herschel Jackson.

The Spring Hill Band of 1894 is pictured on the grounds of the Spring Hill Methodist Church. From left to right are (first row) Sid Woodward, Virgil Smith, Treva Lamkin, Dr. Lamkin, Jet Lamkin, and Lonnie Lamkin; (second row) Henry Evans, Will Vanhook, Dick Reese, Dr. Bob Byassee, and Newt Reese Sr.

Members of the Oakton Band in 1925 were, from left to right, Jack Young on the bass fiddle; Gilbert Jones on saxophone; Jim Wiley Grimmitt on the piano; Moss Jones on drums; and Phillip Bussey, Thomas Woodrow, Carl Williams, and James Brown in the quartet.

This 1956 picture is of the Clinton Community Service Club, organized to serve dinners to bereaved families on the day of the funeral and to give aid to the sick. Later the club helped with care of the African American cemeteries. From left to right are (first row) Lorene Crume, Eva Dickerson, Rosie Dillard, Nell Sherfield, MayBelle Coneal, Julia Hughes, Elizabeth King, and Lena Evans; (second row) Lillian Elliott, Lovies Henry, Mattie Dunaway, Katie May DeBerry, Ola May Jordan, Jessie Lee DeBose, Eva May Weatherspoon, Cressie Emerson, Norine Weatherspoon, Luline Smith, Mary E. McClain, and Ola Lee Thorp; (third row) Will Patrick, Willie L. Dunaway, Rev. William Elliot, and Buster Jones.

This is a picture of a hanging at the 1878 Hickman County jail. This jail was located on the corner of Mayfield Highway 58 and the east side of South Washington Street. This jail served until 1910–1911, when a new jail was built on an adjoining lot. The 1910 jail served until 1992, when it was declared substandard and ceased to be used as a jail.

The above picture was taken as the 1918 tornado bore down on Hickman County. The gray mass in the middle of the picture is the tornado itself. The picture below was taken after the tornado, showing some of the destruction in its wake. It struck the Oakwood community and traveled southwest for a few miles. It then veered toward Clinton and crossed the Illinois Central Railroad tracks just south of the station. The Cypress community and the Pleasant Valley community both sustained damage and deaths.

During the 1960s and 1970s in the month of December, the merchants of Clinton donated prizes to be drawn every Saturday afternoon on the courthouse square. When customers bought merchandise at a store, they received tickets that they printed their name on and put in a large drum in the courthouse. Santa came Saturday afternoon and helped draw winning tickets from the drum. Everyone in the county wanted to be in Clinton on those afternoons.

Looking from the bluffs in Columbus-Belmont State Park, one can see the Mississippi River and the boats, barges, and tows as they pass. Where the land juts out with trees and the beach is sandy-looking is Wolf Island. The old channel is to the right of the island. The fence keeps tourists from getting too close to the cliffs and falling over the edge.

This house, built in 1852, was once used as a hospital during the Civil War by both the Confederate and Union soldiers. In 1992, the structure had to be moved to a new location so in the future it would not plummet into the Mississippi River. It is now a Civil War Museum where people can view displays of Civil War artifacts, a replica of a hospital scene, Civil War uniforms, and weapons.

Civil War Days is celebrated annually on the second weekend in October at the park. Civil War Days is held to commemorate the Civil War battle that was directly across the river from Columbus in Belmont, Missouri. Today reenactors come, both Confederate and Union, to stage the battle in the fortifications at Columbus-Belmont State Park. The other events include historic and period arts, food vendors, a Confederate training camp, a Civil War wedding, and a formal ball. On Sunday, church services are held in the park.

In 1899, a group of about 20 women organized themselves into the Magazine Club. It soon changed its name to the Clinton Woman's Club. In 1917, with only 9 books and $23, the club opened Hickman County's first public library. Shown above is the house that, in 1936, Daisy Reed Craig deeded to the club to use as a library and clubrooms. In 1972, with the help of the Lions Club, the Woman's Club erected the building below. The club meets on the lower floor while the upper floor houses the Hickman County Memorial Library.

The Hickman County Museum can be found on East Clay Street across from the Clinton Bank. It is housed in a dwelling that was donated by the descendants of Henry Cruse Watson in 1994. It houses items of generations past and is open to the public on Wednesday and Saturday afternoons. Also groups, such as classes of schoolchildren, can make arrangements for tours. The Hickman County Museum Annex was acquired in 1998 and is adjacent to the museum.

*Five*

# SCHOOLS
## FROM MOTHER'S MORNING OUT TO MARVIN COLLEGE

When the elementary school burned in 1982, the historical columns were saved. A memorial was built on the southwest corner of the elementary school lot and the columns placed there.

This is a class of Frances Warren's Mother's Morning Out students. On Tuesday morning, for many years, Warren and a few helpers entertained children under school age for a couple of hours, giving moms a little break. Warren was warmly referred to as "Miss Frances" by most of the county. Miss Frances is seated on the left of the picture.

During the flood of 1927, the Columbus School was completely destroyed. This is a picture of the new Columbus School that was built in 1928. It was the home of the elementary and high school students until 1937, when the 11th and 12th grades were consolidated with Clinton. In 1948, the 9th and 10th grades were consolidated. The last eight grades were transported to Clinton, and the building was torn down.

This is a picture of the old Beelerton High School. Beelerton was first a graded school that began about 1876. Not until 1916 did it become a high school. In 1967, it closed and the children were bused to Hickman County High School and Elementary School.

This is a group of Hickman County public schoolteachers in 1919. From left to right are (first row) Addie Bone, Maybelle Seay, Docie Jones, Ina Bellow, and Lillian Seay; (second row) Mary Barry, Nettie Samuels, Gladys Blair, Evie Jackson, May Sumner, and Warner Willey; (third row) unidentified, Ila Vanpool, Bessie Byassee, and Dean Jackson. Several of them taught in the one- and two-room schools across the county.

1909

The Clinton College, a Baptist school, operated in Clinton from 1874 to 1913. In 1880, Amanda Hicks became president and worked diligently to help this school further the education of many students. West and east wings were added, and the campus layout included a three-story brick girls dormitory, two boys cottages, and a tennis court. An "audience hall" on the second floor had a seating capacity of 600. In 1917, the property was sold to the Hickman County Board of Education, and it was used for the Clinton High School from 1918 to 1935, when it was torn down.

Clinton Central High School was built about 1938. The white columns seen in the photograph came from the old building that was occupied by Clinton College. That building was torn down in 1937 to make way for a new building. In 1959, it became Hickman County Elementary School with grades one through eight. The picture on the opposite page shows the school building before it burned in 1998.

This is the Hickman County Elementary School as it was before July 1998, when it burned. The historical columns of the school were saved and a memorial built on a corner of the school property.

This new school building that was constructed in 1999 after the fire still educates the children of Hickman County today. A new physical education facility was built in 2001.

The Hickman County High School is shown as it stands today. In 1959, a new school was built in the north part of Clinton. It was to serve the entire county's population of high school students. It had been consolidated with the high schools in Columbus and Fulgham. The school has had several remodeling projects in the past years.

Education in Hickman County was left to the one- and two-room schools for 100 years or more. The Deweese School was opened around 1880 and sat about one mile from the community of Oakton on land deeded by Jesse Deweese to the Board of Education. This picture was taken in 1930 with Ocie King as the teacher. From left to right are (first row) Mildred Mills, Evelyn Bragg, John Robert Smith, Faye Cox, and Wilma Overly; (second row) Josephene Mills, Hilda Overly, Elsie Stewart, Edith Cox, and Edna Mae Rushton; (third row) Doris Stewart, Clovis Mills, and Eugene Bragg.

These are eighth-grade graduates of Sunshine Hill Colored School, located in Columbus. Children went to Sunshine Hill through the 1950s. Van Farmer bought the building and made a dwelling of it. The building later burned. The students from left to right are Rosie Nell Deboe Harper, Johnson Webster Johnson, Annie Louise Campbell, and Hazel Johnson Litsey.

This picture was made in November 1912 at Hundley School. The school was said to have been educating children in the late 1870s or 1880s. It was located south of the Fulgham community on what is now New Bethel Road. In 1937, the board of education decided to transfer the pupils to Fulgham and to close the school because of the low attendance rate.

The Mount Pleasant School was one of the 60 or so one- and two-room schools located in Hickman County. It was in the eastern part of the county across the road from the Mount Pleasant Church. Mount Pleasant was educating pupils in 1889 and continued until 1939, when the students were moved to Fulgham School.

This is a picture of Gore School in 1910. This one-room school was located in the southwestern part of the county on the road to Harmony Church. In 1938, the school building was completely destroyed by fire and the school was not rebuilt. The pupils were bused to Clinton to school. No one has identified anyone in the picture.

Fulgham School was built somewhere around 1914. It evidently had all 12 grades since Evie Jackson, a well-known teacher, was in the first graduating class of 1918. A new brick building was erected in 1937 and educated pupils until the schools were consolidated and the students transferred to the Hickman County High School. This is a picture of a class in 1939. From left to right are (first row) Alpha Mae Burgess, William Clark, Louise Armbruster, Johnnie Doris House, and Howard "Shorty" Bugg; (second row) Rebecca Elliott, Wallace Tyner, Lorraine Johns, and Alben Nichols.

Visit us at
arcadiapublishing.com

.....................................

CPSIA information can be obtained
at www.ICGtesting.com
Printed in the USA
LVHW062349150722
723645LV00005B/156